Maths 1

Counting Forwards

A Count from 23 to 68 in 5s. _____

Count from 13 to 77 in 8s. _____

Count from 35 to 91 in 7s. _____

Count from 1.5 to 5.0 in 0.5s. _____

Count from $2\frac{1}{2}$ to 6 in $\frac{1}{2}$s. _____

Count from 1.0 to 2.75 in 0.25s. _____

B Write the missing numbers.

$$
\begin{array}{r}
6\,\square \\
+\ 1\ 8 \\
\hline
8\ 6
\end{array}
\qquad
\begin{array}{r}
5\,\square \\
-\ 2\ 7 \\
\hline
2\ 9
\end{array}
\qquad
\begin{array}{r}
\square\,3 \\
\times\quad 8 \\
\hline
2\ 6\ 4
\end{array}
\qquad
\begin{array}{r}
7\ 9 \\
+\ 2\,\square \\
\hline
1\ 0\ 3
\end{array}
\qquad
\begin{array}{r}
1\,\square \\
9\,\overline{)\,1\ 2\ 6}
\end{array}
$$

$$
\begin{array}{r}
2\,\square\,8 \\
+3\ 5\ 7 \\
\hline
6\ 0\ 5
\end{array}
\qquad
\begin{array}{r}
1\ 9\,\square \\
\times\quad 4 \\
\hline
7\ 8\ 4
\end{array}
\qquad
\begin{array}{r}
6\ 2\ 9 \\
-3\,\square\,5 \\
\hline
2\ 5\ 4
\end{array}
\qquad
\begin{array}{r}
1\ 7\ 6 \\
\times\quad 5 \\
\hline
8\,\square\,0
\end{array}
\qquad
\begin{array}{r}
1\,\square\,4 \\
6\,\overline{)\,8\ 0\ 4}
\end{array}
$$

Angles

C Write **R** under each **right** angle, **O** under each **obtuse** angle and **A** under each **acute** angle.

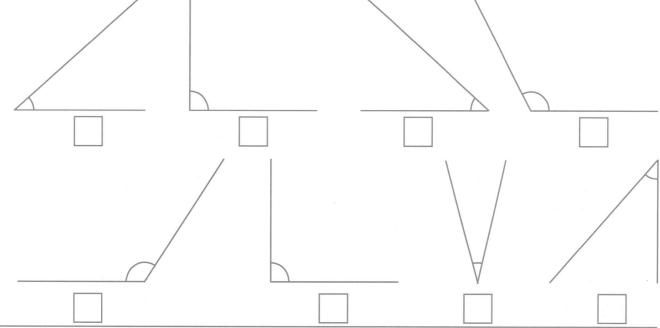

D Write **+**, **−**, **x** or **÷** in each square to make the answer correct.

1   7 ☐ 8 = 56   36 ☐ 9 = 4   5 ☐ 20 = 100

2   117 ☐ 86 = 31   129 ☐ 26 = 155   144 ☐ 12 = 12

3   9 ☐ 9 = 81   163 ☐ 49 = 212   62 ☐ 24 = 38

Witches' Spells

The sky is dark, the stars are bright
The moon is shining too
Inside a cave the witches meet
To mix their favourite brew.

They light a fire, and when it flames
They fetch a big black pot;
They fill it up with lizards' blood,
Then wait until it's hot.

Each one has brought a magic charm
To put into the stew,
A spider's web, a fairy's wing,
A beetle's leg, or two.

They take a stick, and bending low
They stir the mixture round.
They rub their fingers, old and cramped
And stamp upon the ground.

Their wizened faces grin with glee,
As round the pot they prance,
Their sharp eyes glisten in the dark,
Their cloaks swirl as they dance.

They drink, and then into the sky,
On broomsticks, swift and light,
They cackle hoarsely as they fly,
And soon are out of sight.

A. Nightingale

A

1 Name the charms the witches put into the pot. _____

2 What kind of charms would you choose? Why? _____

3 Why do you think the witches were meeting?_____

4 How does the poet describe the witches? _____
_____

5 How do you know the witches were happy when they danced around the pot?
_____

6 Look carefully in the poem to find synonyms for each of these words:
cauldron _____   prance _____   spell _____   shine _____

Idioms

B
Write a sentence that shows you know what each of these **idioms** means.
The first one is done for you.

1 red-handed   The thief was caught red-handed stealing the jewels.

2 the lion's share   _____

3 to be in the pink _____

4 get cold feet   _____

5 in hot water   _____

6 a fish out of water _____

Maths 2

Multiplying Decimals

A Multiply these. The first two are done for you.

$$\begin{array}{r} 5.3 \\ \times\ 4 \\ \hline 21.2 \end{array} \qquad \begin{array}{r} 7.6 \\ \times\ 7 \\ \hline 53.2 \end{array}$$

$$\begin{array}{r} 3.8 \\ \times\ 3 \\ \hline \end{array} \qquad \begin{array}{r} 6.7 \\ \times\ 5 \\ \hline \end{array} \qquad \begin{array}{r} 9.5 \\ \times\ 8 \\ \hline \end{array} \qquad \begin{array}{r} 7.8 \\ \times\ 6 \\ \hline \end{array} \qquad \begin{array}{r} 5.9 \\ \times\ 9 \\ \hline \end{array}$$

$$\begin{array}{r} 6.9 \\ \times\ 4 \\ \hline \end{array} \qquad \begin{array}{r} 8.4 \\ \times\ 7 \\ \hline \end{array} \qquad \begin{array}{r} 7.5 \\ \times\ 6 \\ \hline \end{array} \qquad \begin{array}{r} 5.6 \\ \times\ 9 \\ \hline \end{array} \qquad \begin{array}{r} 9.8 \\ \times\ 5 \\ \hline \end{array}$$

Pie Chart

B There are 40 boys in a sports club who voted on their favourite games.

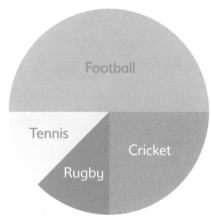

1 What fraction of the boys preferred

football ☐   cricket ☐   rugby ☐   tennis ☐?

2 What percentage of the boys liked

football ☐%   cricket ☐%   rugby ☐%   tennis ☐%?

3 Write the number of boys who liked

cricket ☐   tennis ☐   rugby ☐   football ☐.

Ordering Numbers

C Write out these numbers in order, starting with the smallest.

1	53402	5897	327482	896	272284
	_____	_____	_____	_____	_____
2	40200	39640	4200	42000	39650
	_____	_____	_____	_____	_____
3	76543	7812	76541	67541	76450
	_____	_____	_____	_____	_____
4	1578	7518	8751	5875	7508
	_____	_____	_____	_____	_____
5	8800	8008	8080	880	8000
	_____	_____	_____	_____	_____

Language 3

Simple Machines

A Choose words from the word box to fill in correctly the seven blanks.

shorter	inclined	easier	machine	longer	ramp	force

Machines can help people to do work. In the pictures in part c, you can see that the _____ makes the man's work _____. The ramp is a simple _____ called an inclined plane. An _____ plane makes the work less difficult by reducing the amount of force required to push a load. Using a ramp, the man pushes the lawnmower with less force than if he tried to lift the lawnmower. By using the ramp, the man pushes the lawnmower a _____ distance, but with less force. If he lifted the lawnmower on to the Land Rover he would move it a _____ distance, but he would use a lot more _____.

B Today ramps are used to help people in wheelchairs move around more easily. Write the names of three places where ramps could be used in your area.

1 _____

2 _____

3 _____

C Look at these two pictures.

1

2

1 On which ramp would the lawnmower have to be pushed farthest to get on to the Land Rover? Number ☐

2 On which ramp will the smallest use of force be needed to roll the lawnmower on to the Land Rover? Number ☐

3 The angle of the ramp affects the amount of force needed to move the lawnmower. How?

_____

_____

Language 4

Rhyming Words

A Among these fifteen words are five sets of **rhyming words** – three words in each set. Write out the five sets.

taught	earth	plate	view	shows	birth	hose	sort
wait	goes	worth	fête	queue	brought	crew	

_____   _____   _____   _____   _____

_____   _____   _____   _____   _____

_____   _____   _____   _____   _____

Incorrect Sentences

B Write these sentences correctly.

1 There is a lot of high mountains in Switzerland.

2 My sister, Samantha, is about a year older than me.

3 Carol, Laura and Errol was waiting for the school bus.

4 I shared my chocolates between Ruth, Neil and Shena.

5 "We didn't do nothing wrong," cried Iain.

6 Wilma ran good in the race.

More Joining Words

C Complete these six sentences with a suitable **joining word** chosen from the box.

when	although	wherever	because	but	until

1 The faithful labrador followed the farmer _____ he went.
2 Our plane couldn't take off _____ the fog lifted.
3 Bob wasn't able to play rugby _____ he had pulled a muscle.
4 We were walking near the Post Office _____ we saw the crash.
5 We pushed and pulled at the door _____ couldn't open it.
6 We enjoyed the film _____ we had seen it before.

Spellings

D In this list of twenty-four words there are ten words spelt incorrectly. Write them correctly in the spaces below.

argument	beautifull	accept	excitment	because	century	caterpiller	equator
flavour	interupt	library	marvelous	necessary	occasion	differant	sanwich
although	opposite	cupboard	sucessful	straight	peculiar	sattelite	neice

_____   _____   _____   _____   _____

_____   _____   _____   _____   _____

Maths 3

Missing Numbers

A Write what the two missing numbers could be.

☐ + ☐ = 16   ☐ − ☐ = 15   ☐ x ☐ = 24

☐ ÷ ☐ = 6   ☐ + ☐ = 37   ☐ − ☐ = 41

☐ x ☐ = 56   ☐ ÷ ☐ = 11   ☐ x ☐ = 72

More Multiplying Decimals

B Multiply these. The first two are done for you.

```
   28.5          38.6
x     2       x     7
-------       -------
   57.0         270.2
```

```
   46.3          35.6          26.7          55.4          28.9
x     4       x     8       x     6       x     7       x     5
-------       -------       -------       -------       -------
```

```
   63.6          75.8          39.3          49.9          86.4
x     6       x     7       x     9       x     5       x     8
-------       -------       -------       -------       -------
```

C Complete these four symmetrical shapes.

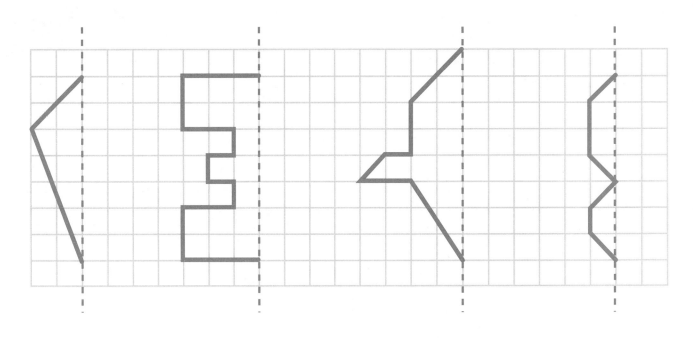

8

Language 5

Vocabulary

A Write the word in each line which stands for all the other words.

1 football cricket tennis game rugby hockey   _____

2 bungalow flat house apartment dwelling cottage   _____

3 settee table wardrobe armchair bookcase furniture   _____

4 train hovercraft ferry aircraft transport coach taxi   _____

5 pound lira yen currency dollar escudo mark   _____

6 spanner hacksaw pincers tools screwdriver hammer   _____

Past Tense Verbs

B Rewrite these five sentences in the **past tense**.

1 Charlotte wears a gold locket round her neck. _____

_____

2 The London train leaves the station at 8.30 am. _____

_____

3 The football match attracts a crowd of nearly fifty thousand. _____

_____

4 The cat creeps through the long grass towards the squirrel. _____

_____

5 I am so excited, I feel like jumping over the moon. _____

_____

Dial-a-word – Spelling and Vocabulary

C Build new words by writing **dis** before the letters in the small circles. Make sure the words match the clues.

ease   agree   cuss   cover   **dis**   trict   play   aster   turb

1 a show or exhibition _____

2 to find out about something _____

3 illness, sickness _____

4 a very serious accident, a tragedy _____

5 to talk sensibly about something _____

6 to interrupt, to upset _____

7 a part of a town, county or country _____

8 to have different views or opinions_____

Homophones

D **Homophones** are words that have the same sound but different meanings and spellings. For each of these eight words write another word which sounds exactly the same but is spelt differently.

beech _____   medal _____   sight   _____   waist _____

right _____   hole _____   stationary _____   aloud _____

Maths 4

Brackets First!

A Don't forget to work out the sums in the **brackets** first. The first one is done for you.

1 3 + (4 x 5) = 3 + 20 = 23

2 6 + (3 x 8) = 6 + ☐ = ☐

3 (6 x 7) + 9 = ☐ + 9 = ☐

4 (8 + 4) x 8 = ☐ x 8 = ☐

5 9 + (24 ÷ 6) = 9 + ☐ = ☐

6 (42 ÷ 3) – 12 = ☐ – 12 = ☐

7 4 x (36 ÷ 4) = 4 x ☐ = ☐

Schools' Football Graph

B Below is the record of the football matches played between eight school teams, showing the matches won.

	0	5	10	15
Podgate				
Woodstock				
Leigh				
Burford				
Eccleston				
Redhill				
Mellor				
Lymm				

1 Which team won the most matches? _____

2 Which team won the fewest matches? _____

3 Which teams won the same number of matches?

_____

4 Which two teams together won the same number of matches as Woodstock?

_____

5 How many more matches did Podgate win than Burford? _____

6 Which two teams together won as many matches as Mellor and Woodstock put together?

_____

Number Patterns

C Write the next **three** numbers in each of the four patterns.

4, 5, 7, 10, ☐, ☐, ☐   56, 50, 54, ☐, ☐, ☐

–3, –10, –17, ☐, ☐, ☐   2, 9, 16, 23, ☐, ☐, ☐

Fill in the two boxes in this number pattern.

1, 3, 7, 15, ☐, ☐, 127

What is happening to make the numbers increase? _____

10

Science 1

You and Your Bones

A Ask a grown-up to help you to measure these bones in your body. You will need a tape measure. Write your answers in the spaces.

1 Length of lower leg from knee to ankle _____ cm.

2 Distance around your wrist _____ cm.

3 Distance around skull _____ cm.

4 Length of foot from tip of big toe to heel _____ cm.

5 Distance from top of arm to centre of neck _____ cm.

6 Length of thigh bone from knee to hip joint _____ cm.

7 Distance around ankle _____ cm.

8 Length of upper arm _____ cm.

9 Length of lower arm _____ cm.

10 Length of third finger _____ cm.

skull

jawbone

shoulder blade

collarbone

breastbone

upper arm

rib

lower arm

spine (backbone)

wrist

hip bone

finger bones

hip joint

thigh bone

kneecap

lower leg

shin bone

ankle

B Ask a grown-up if you can measure **their** bones so you can compare the measurements with yours.

C Use an encyclopaedia or reference book to find the technical name for each of these bones.

breastbone _____   collarbone _____

thigh bone _____   shin bone _____

shoulder blade _____   jawbone _____

kneecap _____

Maths 5

Missing Numbers

A Write the missing number.

1 $40 - 19 = 11 + \boxed{}$ 2 $52 - 18 = 14 + \boxed{}$

3 $76 - 42 = 17 + \boxed{}$ 4 $67 - 26 = 19 + \boxed{}$

5 $53 - 28 = 6 + \boxed{}$ 6 $81 - 55 = 5 + \boxed{}$

Triangles

B These four shapes are **triangles**. Use the word box to help you to choose their names. Why are they different from each other? Write down your findings. Remember angles and lengths of sides.

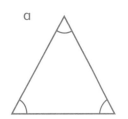 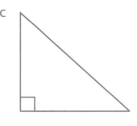 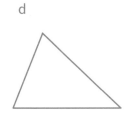

a   b   c   d

1 Name of triangle _____   _____   _____   _____

2 Your findings   a _____

b _____

c _____

d _____

right-angled   isosceles   scalene   equilateral

Comparing Fractions

C Which is bigger?

$\dfrac{1}{3}$ or $\dfrac{1}{4}$ = $\boxed{}$ $\dfrac{3}{4}$ or $\dfrac{5}{8}$ = $\boxed{}$ $\dfrac{13}{20}$ or $\dfrac{7}{10}$ = $\boxed{}$

$\dfrac{7}{10}$ or $\dfrac{4}{5}$ = $\boxed{}$ $\dfrac{2}{3}$ or $\dfrac{7}{12}$ = $\boxed{}$ $\dfrac{3}{5}$ or $\dfrac{2}{3}$ = $\boxed{}$ $\dfrac{3}{4}$ or $\dfrac{7}{10}$ = $\boxed{}$

$\dfrac{2}{3}$ or $\dfrac{5}{8}$ = $\boxed{}$ $\dfrac{3}{4}$ or $\dfrac{5}{6}$ = $\boxed{}$ $\dfrac{9}{10}$ or $\dfrac{7}{8}$ = $\boxed{}$ $\dfrac{3}{5}$ or $\dfrac{13}{20}$ = $\boxed{}$

D More Brackets First

1 $(6 + 4) \times (12 - 6)$ = $\boxed{} \times \boxed{} = \boxed{}$

2 $(12 - 4) \times (12 \div 3)$ = $\boxed{} \times \boxed{} = \boxed{}$

3 $(8 \times 6) \div (18 \div 3)$ = $\boxed{} \div \boxed{} = \boxed{}$

4 $(21 \div 7) \times (81 \div 9)$ = $\boxed{} \times \boxed{} = \boxed{}$

5 $(9 \times 8) \div (2 \times 12)$ = $\boxed{} \div \boxed{} = \boxed{}$

Language 6

Steeplejack

A steeplejack's life is full of danger and excitement, as usually he works very high above the ground. He builds and repairs tall chimneys which are sometimes constructed of brick and sometimes of steel. He also repairs church spires and steeples.

A chimney may be as high as 180 metres. The spire of Salisbury Cathedral is about 123 metres high. A steeplejack cannot afford to be clumsy. He must always work cautiously and can never relax. One slip and he will fall to his death.

The steeplejack must have many skills. Besides building with bricks and mortar, he welds and rivets metal. He uses an oxy-acetylene cutter and he paints. He repairs the lights which are fixed to chimneys to warn aircraft. He may use explosives to demolish a chimney which is no longer wanted. His greatest skill is the ability to do the work high above ground, where there is no room for any mistake.

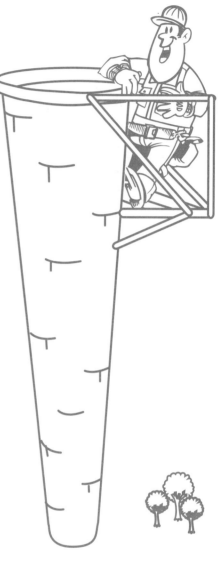

Weather can be a bad enemy to a steeplejack. Sudden winds could sweep him off the chimney. In a strong wind he can only sit down and edge his way to the ladder and safety. Sometimes he wears a breathing mask when he is repairing a chimney in case the wind blows poisonous fumes into his face. Ice and snow make the scaffolding very slippery. During a rainstorm, lightning may strike the chimney and give him a severe electric shock. Truly he works with danger!

D. Newton and D. Smith

From They work with danger

1 Give three reasons for not wanting to be a steeplejack.

_____

_____

_____

2 In your opinion, which talents are the most necessary for a steeplejack to survive?

_____

3 How can the weather be a big problem for the steeplejack?

_____

4 Occasionally the steeplejack wears a breathing mask. Why?

_____

5 Find synonyms in the extract for these words:

mends _____   flatten _____   unexpected _____   peril _____

6 Imagine you are on top of a tall chimney. Describe how you might feel being up there!

_____

_____

_____

_____

Maths 6

Co-ordinates

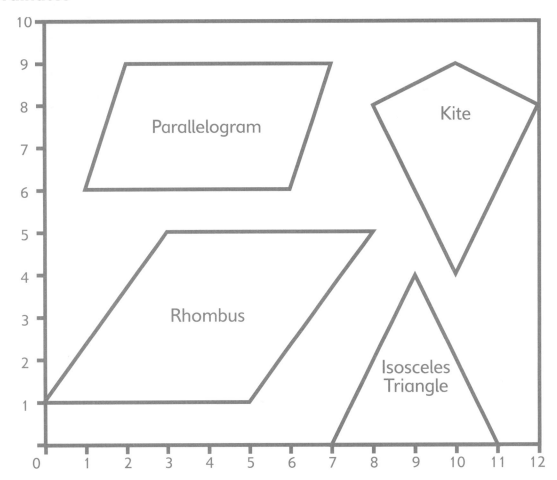

A Write the co-ordinates of each of the four shapes.

Rhombus: (__ , __) (__ , __) (__ , __) (__ , __)

Isosceles triangle: (__ , __) (__ , __) (__ , __)

Kite: (__ , __) (__ , __) (__ , __) (__ , __)

Parallelogram: (__ , __) (__ , __) (__ , __) (__ , __)

Problems

B 1 A train leaves at 11.55am. The journey takes 1 hour 50 minutes. What time does it arrive? _____

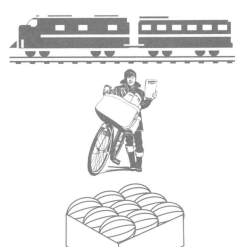

2 Ahmed works $37\frac{1}{2}$ hours in a five-day week. How long does he work each day? _____

3 A paperboy takes 1 hour 20 minutes to deliver his papers. How long does he work in a seven-day week? _____

4 Find the average weight of 2.6kg, 4.9kg, 6.5kg and 3.6kg.

_____

5 Nine boxes hold 338.4kg of melons. How much does each box hold? _____

MORE HOMEWORK BOOK 4 ANSWERS

Note for users

Taking an interest in the child's work is of great importance. Take every opportunity to praise work that is correct, and offer help and advice where the child experiences difficulty. Make sure that the child understands the instructions that introduce each exercise. Some children experience more difficulty with the instructions than with the work itself.

There are advantages in allowing the child to mark his or her own work. This informs the child of the correct answer in cases where mistakes have occurred. It is important to look again at answers that are wrong and for the child to discover why an answer is incorrect so that he or she can learn as a result of the error.

Where a weakness is revealed, further similar exercises can be provided to give the child more practice and confidence.

A child should not be expected to undertake too much work in a short time. The exercises should be well spaced out so that the last pages are being worked towards the end of the appropriate school year.

Language 1   page 2

A   1 and   2 because   3 so   4 while, and
    5 because   6 if

B   1 herself
    2 themselves
    3 myself
    4 ourselves
    5 himself
    6 yourself

C   *Variable answers*

D   1 to
    2 over, into
    3 across, in
    4 among
    5 against, on

Maths 1   page 3

A

23	28	33	38	43	48
53	58	63	68		
13	21	29	37	45	53
61	69	77			
35	42	49	56	63	70
77	84	91			
1.5	2.0	2.5	3.0	3.5	4.0
4.5	5.0				
$2\frac{1}{2}$	3	$3\frac{1}{2}$	4	$4\frac{1}{2}$	5
$5\frac{1}{2}$	6				
1.0	1.25	1.50	1.75	2.0	2.25
2.50	2.75				

B

8	6	3	4	4
4	6	7	8	3

C

A	R	A	O
O	R	A	A

D

1	×	÷	×
2	–	+	÷
3	×	+	–

Language 2   page 4

A   1 Spider's web, fairy's wing, beetle's leg or two
    2 *Variable answers*
    3 To mix their favourite brew
    4 They had old and cramped fingers, wizened faces, sharp eyes that glistened and swirling cloaks.
    5 Their faces grinned with glee as they pranced around the pot.
    6 pot   dance   charm   glisten

B   *Variable answers*

Maths 2   page 5

A

11.4	33.5	76.0	46.8	53.1
27.6	58.8	45.0	50.4	49.0

B   1 $\frac{1}{2}$ football $\frac{1}{4}$ cricket $\frac{1}{8}$ rugby $\frac{1}{8}$ tennis
    2 50% football   25% cricket $12\frac{1}{2}$% rugby $12\frac{1}{2}$% tennis
    3 10 cricket   5 tennis   5 rugby   20 football

C

1	896	5897	53402	272284	327482
2	4200	39640	39650	40200	42000
3	7812	67541	76450	76541	76543
4	1578	5875	7508	7518	8751
5	880	8000	8008	8080	8800

Language 3   page 6

A   ramp, easier, machine, inclined, longer, shorter, force

B   *Variable answers but could include:* access to shops, library, doctor's surgery, cinema, house, etc.

C   1 Picture 2   2 Picture 2
    3 The steeper the ramp, the more force will be needed.

Language 4 — Page 7

A

taught	earth	plate	view	shows
sort	birth	wait	queue	hose
brought	worth	fête	crew	goes

B
1 There are a lot of high mountains in Switzerland.
2 My sister, Samantha, is about a year older than I.
3 Carol, Laura and Errol were waiting for the school bus.
4 I shared my chocolates among Ruth, Neil and Shena.
5 "We didn't do anything wrong," cried Iain.
6 Wilma ran well in the race.

C
1 wherever   2 until   3 because
4 when   5 but   6 although

D

beautiful	excitement	caterpillar	interrupt	marvellous
different	sandwich	successful	satellite	niece

Maths 3 — page 8

A *Variable answers*

B

| 185.2 | 284.8 | 160.2 | 387.8 | 144.5 |
| 381.6 | 530.6 | 353.7 | 249.5 | 691.2 |

C

Language 5 — page 9

A
1 game   2 dwelling   3 furniture
4 transport   5 currency   6 tools

B
1 Charlotte wore a gold locket round her neck.
2 The London train left the station at 8.30 am.
3 The football match attracted a crowd of nearly fifty thousand.
4 The cat crept through the long grass towards the squirrel.
5 I was so excited, I felt like jumping over the moon.

C
1 display   2 discover   3 disease
4 disaster   5 discuss   6 disturb
7 district   8 disagree

D

| beach | meddle | site | waste |
| write | whole | stationery | allowed |

Maths 4 — page 10

A
2 24, 30   3 42, 51   4 12, 96
5 4, 13   6 14, 2   7 9, 36

B
1 Podgate   2 Burford
3 Redhill, Lymm   4 Burford, Mellor
5 8 more   6 Podgate, Burford

C
14, 19, 25   48, 52, 46
−24, −31, −38   30, 37, 44
31, 63

The previous number is doubled and one is added.

Science 1 — page 11

A *Variable answers*

B *Variable answers*

C

sternum	scapula
tibia	femur
clavicle	mandible
patella	

Maths 5 — page 12

A
1 10   2 20   3 17   4 22   5 19   6 21

B
1 a equilateral b isosceles c right-angled d scalene
2 *Variable answers*

C

1/3	3/4	7/10	
4/5	2/3	2/3	3/4
2/3	5/6	9/10	13/20

D
1 $10 \times 6 = 60$ 2 $8 \times 4 = 32$
3 $48 \div 6 = 8$ 4 $3 \times 9 = 27$
5 $72 \div 24 = 3$

Language 6 — page 13

1 *Variable answers but could include:* danger, working high above ground, bad weather.

2 *Variable answers but could include:* caution, alertness, multi-skilled, not afraid of heights.

3 Sudden winds could upset balance; heavy rain, snow or ice could cause slippery surfaces; lightning could strike

4 In case the wind blows poisonous fumes into his face when he is repairing a chimney.

5 repairs demolish sudden danger

6 *Variable answers*

Maths 6 — page 14

A

Rhombus:	(0,1) (3,5) (8,5) (5,1)
Isosceles triangle:	(7,0) (9,4) (11,0)
Kite:	(10,4) (8,8) (10,9) (12,8)
Parallelogram:	(1,6) (2,9) (7,9) (6,6)

B
1 1.45pm   2 $7\frac{1}{2}$hrs
3 9hrs 20mins   4 4.4kg
5 37.6kg

Language 7 — page 15

A
1 discovered   2 illustrated
3 survived   4 treated
5 prepare   6 disturb
7 decide   8 translated

B *Variable answers, but should mean:*

succeed	remember	awake	expensive
enemy	rough	attack	help
polite	careless	borrow	retreat
refuse	maximum	wrong	arrive

C
1 Christina asked whether the train to Harrogate had gone.
2 Grandad inquired if anyone had seen his walking stick.
3 Dr Knight told Gail he was sure the medicine would soon put her right.
4 Uncle Robert asked Kay to help him to carry a roll of velvet.
5 Ms Down snapped at Ella saying she wasn't pleased with her and she must work harder.

D *Variable answers*

Maths 7 — page 16

A

| 3 | | 8 | | 7 | | 4 | | 4 |
| | 3 | | 8 | | 5 | | 9 | |

B
1 a 9 cubes   b 18 cubes
2 16 cubes
3 a 45cm³ b 32cm³ c 84cm³

C

| 1 0.19 | 0.48 | 0.14 | 0.15 | 0.07 |
| 2 0.27 | 0.92 | 0.15 | 0.54 | 0.36 |

Language 8   page 17

A
1 protractor   2 prove
3 probable   4 problem
5 provoke   6 protect
7 prosper   8 provide

B *Variable answers*

C
1 Paul whispered, "I can see the thrush feeding its young."

2 "Come here at once!" he shouted.

3 She said very quietly, "I have something to tell you."

4 "That's a clever idea," Andy said. "We'll see if it works on the CD Writer."

5 "This TV doesn't work," the elderly man grumbled, "so I've brought it back."

D
1 fined, licence   2 ewe
3 their, there   4 pain, muscle
5 threw, rows

E
1 disconnect   impossible   mistrust   unfriendly
2 invisible   disobey   irregular   impatient
3 illegal   unfasten   disappear   misfortune
4 incorrect   impolite   unclear   unpleasant

Maths 8   page 18

A
1 2.57   3.63   5.16   6.24   2.69
2 2.176   0.747   1.699   3.045   3.257

B
1 8732   9654   7432   8650
2 2100   7530   9860   9710

C

1	0.68	2	1.77
	0.60		0.65
	0.82		1.20
	1.64		0.16
Total	3.74	Total	3.78
3	2.37	4	3.33
	0.59		2.37
	0.19		2.68
	5.97		1.65
Total	9.12	Total	10.03

D
1 Height 2cm   2 Height 3cm
   Base 4cm   Base 6cm
   Area 4cm²   Area 9cm²

3 Height 4cm
   Base 3cm
   Area 6 cm²

Language 9   page 19

1 Lullabyed softly

2 Tied up their heads and bound their eardrums

3 They made a giant clothes-peg to place on Barrington Brown's nose.
It wasn't a success because one huge snore blew it off.

4 Left town in cars and carts

5 frantic   mighty   lullabyed
deafening   ignore

6 *Variable answers*

Science 2   page 20

A *Variable answers*

B
1 sitting
Variable answers but should be based on: you aren't using much energy yet, so the heart pumps normally.

2 jumping on the spot or running on the spot or press-ups
Variable answers but should be based on: the more energy you use the quicker the heart pumps the blood around your body.

C *Variable answers*

Maths 9   page 21

A

25	25 / 100	0.25	25%
20	20 / 100	0.2	20%
10	10 / 100	0.1	10%
5	5 / 100	0.05	5%
4	4 / 100	0.04	4%
2	2 / 100	0.02	2%

B
1 5   2 12   3 7   4 7   5 3.1

C
1 50%   2 250%   3 25%
4 100%   5 75%   6 125%

Language 10   page 22

A
1 golden   musical   poisonous   showery
2 skilful   friendly   accidental   sunny
3 natural   circular   woollen   metallic
4 foolish   beautiful   valuable   watery

B
1 mice   2 glove
3 lose   4 run
5 this   6 thirsty
7 nephew   8 late
9 hand   10 ascend

C
1 punctually
2 regularly
3 softly or quietly
4 incessantly or constantly
5 silently
6 finally

D
1 "I am going to plant some shrubs," explained the gardener.
2 "Have you read any of the Harry Potter books, Gary?" asked his teacher.
3 "Are you going to the cinema on Tuesday?" asked Judy.
4 "The cushion is much too hard for me," complained Grandpa.
5 "The laptop you like is too expensive and you must wait to see how you progress with our desktop," explained Dad.

Maths 10   page 23

A
1 100g   2 42   3 53
4 £4.00   5 2.3

B
1 119
2 Sun, Sat, Fri; *variable answers*
3 17 cars
4 Five; *variable answers*
5 Mon, Tues, Thurs
6 £300

C
1 15   2 £31.35   3 162m
4 105   5 £1.35

Language 11   page 24

1 To carry him on his back

2 He had pity on his old age

3 The old man twisted his legs tightly round Sinbad's neck and nearly choked him.

4 The old man dug his feet into Sinbad's stomach.

5 It gave him fresh strength and he danced and sang.

6 The old man became very happy and loosened his grip on Sinbad's shoulders.

7   lest
faint   wearily   goodwill

8 Sinbad killed him.

9 bottle.

Maths 11 · page 25

A
| 20% | 25% | 45% | 50% | 66% |
| 80% | 75% | 55% | 50% | 34% |

B TOT, MUM

C
1 4
2 9
3 6
4 11
5 27

D
1 30° 45° 25° 60°
2 120° 150° 105°

Language 12 · page 26

A *Variable answers*
B *Variable answers*

Maths 12 · page 27

A
1 Perimeter 18cm Area 8cm^2
2 Perimeter 22cm Area 10cm^2
3 Perimeter 24cm Area 15cm^2

B
1 7p	2 18p	3 2.5m
4 9g	5 80m	6 50kg
7 150m	8 80l	

C

Family ticket	£14.50		£ 5.55
			free
			£ 6.30
Total	£14.50	Total	£11.85
Change	£ 5.50	Change	£ 8.15

	£ 7.00		£16.65
	£ 5.00		£ 2.50
Total	£12.00	Total	£19.15
Change	£ 8.00	Change	85p

Language 7

Forming Verbs from Nouns

A Use **verbs** formed from the nouns in bold type to complete the sentences.

1 **discovery**   Sir Alexander Fleming _____ penicillin.

2 **illustration**   The 'Bird Book' was _____ with beautiful drawings.

3 **survival**   How the soldiers _____ the heat of the desert is a miracle.

4 **treatment**   Tina's cut arm was _____ at the hospital.

5 **preparation**   We have to _____ for the visit of our aunt and uncle.

6 **disturbance**   Grandma is sleeping. Don't _____ her.

7 **decision**   It took Earl a long time to _____ what he wanted to do.

8 **translation**   Our teacher had _____ the Spanish letter into English.

Antonyms

B An **antonym** is opposite in meaning to another word. For example, **noisy** is the antonym of **quiet**. Write the antonyms of these sixteen words.

fail _____	forget _____	asleep _____	cheap _____
friend _____	smooth _____	defend _____	hinder _____
rude _____	cautious _____	lend _____	advance _____
accept _____	minimum _____	correct _____	depart _____

Direct to Indirect Speech

C Change these five sentences from **direct** to **indirect** speech. Here is an example.

Mum said, "Lock the shed when you've finished." [direct speech]

Mum told us to lock the shed when we had finished. [indirect speech]

1 "Has the train to Harrogate gone?" asked Christina.

_____

2 "Has anyone seen my walking stick?" inquired Grandad.

_____

3 "I'm sure this medicine will soon put you right, Gail," said Dr Knight.

_____

4 "Kay," said Uncle Robert, "will you help me to carry this roll of velvet?"

_____

5 "I'm not pleased with you, Ella," snapped Ms Down. "Now work harder!"

_____

Questions

D Here are the answers to different questions. First write a humorous question and then write a serious question for each answer.

1 Over the Swiss Alps.   a _____
   b _____

2 In his football kit.   a _____
   b _____

3 On the banks of the Thames.   a _____
   b _____

4 With a hippopotamus.   a _____
   b _____

5 In a space shuttle.   a _____
   b _____

6 At the hairdresser's.   a _____
   b _____

Maths 7

More Missing Numbers

A

```
  4 5 6        6 □ 6        7 □ 8        8 3 2        9 4 5
+ 2 □ 8      + 2 7 9      - 4 3 7      -  6 □ 2      - 4 □ 6
  6 9 4        9 6 5        3 4 1         1 9 0         4 9 9
```

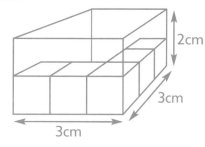

$5\overline{)670}$ with quotient 1□4

$8\overline{)9□4}$ with quotient 1 2 3

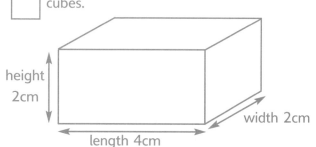

```
    2 3 6            1 □ 7
  x     7          x     8
  1 6 □ 2          1 5 7 6
```

Volume

B

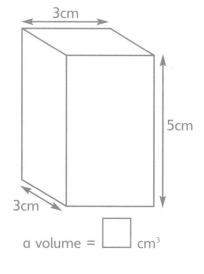

2cm

3cm

3cm

1 a How many 1cm cubes will fit on the bottom?

☐ cubes.

b How 1c, many cubes will fill the whole box?

☐ cubes.

height 2cm

length 4cm

width 2cm

2 How many 1cm cubes would fill this box?

☐ cubes.

3 Find the volume of each of these three cuboids. Remember: Volume = L x W x H.

3cm

5cm

3cm

a volume = ☐ cm³

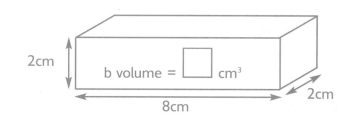

2cm

b volume = ☐ cm³

8cm

2cm

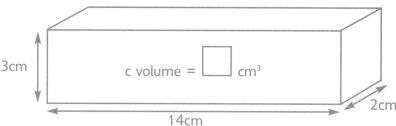

3cm

c volume = ☐ cm³

14cm

2cm

Decimals – Division

C 1 $4\overline{)0.76}$ 2 $\overline{)0.96}$ 6 $\overline{)0.84}$ 5 $\overline{)0.75}$ 9 $\overline{)0.63}$

   2   6 $\overline{)1.62}$ 8 $\overline{)7.36}$ 12 $\overline{)1.80}$ 9 $\overline{)4.86}$ 7 $\overline{)2.52}$

Language 8

More Dial-a-word – Spelling and Vocabulary

A Build new words by writing **pro** before the letters in the small circles.
Make sure the words match the clues.

Circle diagram with centre **pro** surrounded by: voke, ve, sper, tect, bable, tractor, vide, blem

1 used to measure angles _____
2 show that something is true _____
3 likely to happen _____
4 question, difficulty to be solved _____
5 to make someone angry _____
6 to keep safe, to guard _____
7 do well, be successful _____
8 to supply what is needed _____

Verbs and Adverbs

B Write interesting sentences using these pairs of **verbs and adverbs**.

1 staggered clumsily _____
2 stared insolently _____
3 fought bravely _____
4 swerved violently _____
5 waited anxiously _____
6 behaved rudely _____

Spoken Words

C Add the speech marks and other punctuation needed to these sentences.

1 Paul whispered   I can see the thrush feeding its young
2 Come here at once   he shouted
3 She said very quietly   I have something to tell you
4 That's a clever idea   Andy said   We'll see if it works on the CD Writer
5 This TV doesn't work   the elderly man grumbled   so I've brought it back

More Homophones

D Complete these five sentences by choosing the correct word from inside
the brackets.

1 Mrs King was [fined, find] _____ for not paying her TV [license, licence] _____.
2 A female sheep is a [yew, ewe] _____.
3 Where are [their, there] _____ shoes? I saw them over [their, there] _____.
4 Jack had much [pane, pain] _____ when he pulled a [muscle, mussel] _____.
5 Maisie [through, threw] _____ the ball over the [rose, rows] _____ of seats.

Opposites

E Add the correct prefix from the list to each of the sixteen words so that they have the **opposite**
meaning.

in	dis	un	im	il	mis	ir

1 connect _____   possible _____   trust _____   friendly _____
2 visible _____   obey _____   regular_____   patient _____
3 legal _____   fasten _____   appear_____   fortune _____
4 correct _____   polite _____   clear _____   pleasant _____

Maths 8

Decimals – More Division

A 1   2 ⟌ 5.14   4 ⟌ 14.52   7 ⟌ 36.12   11 ⟌ 68.64   12 ⟌ 32.28

    2   3 ⟌ 6.528   3 ⟌ 2.241   5 ⟌ 8.495   7 ⟌ 21.315   4 ⟌ 13.028

B   Write the largest number you can make by using each of these four digits.

1   3 8 2 7 → ☐   6 4 9 5 → ☐   4 3 2 7 → ☐   0 8 5 6 → ☐

2   2 0 1 0 → ☐   5 3 0 7 → ☐   6 0 8 9 → ☐   1 0 7 9 → ☐

Money – Bills

C   Find the total cost of these four shopping bills.

1   4 oranges @ 17p each   = _____

     ½kg bananas @ £1.20/kg   = _____

     250g apples @ £3.28/kg   = _____

     500g grapes @ £3.28/kg   = _____

                     Total _____

2   3 peppers @ 59p each   = _____

     ½kg tomatoes @ £1.30/kg   = _____

     750g pears @ £1.60/kg   = _____

     500g carrots @ 32p/kg   = _____

                     Total _____

3   750g mushrooms @ £3.16/kg   = _____

     ½kg broccoli @ £1.18/kg   = _____

     250g sprouts @ 76p/kg   = _____

     3 pizzas @ £1.99 each   = _____

                     Total _____

4   9 yoghurts @ 37p each   = _____

     3 loaves @ 79p each   = _____

     4 tins of soup @ 67p each   = _____

     3 tins custard @ 55p each   = _____

                     Total _____

Area of Triangles

D   Remember the area of a triangle = ½ base x height or (base x height) ÷ 2.
Find the area of these triangles.

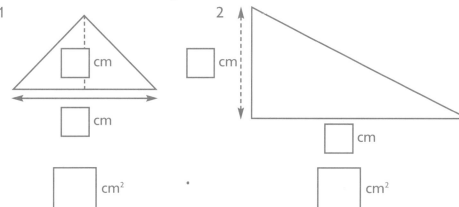

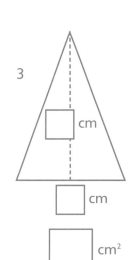

Be Quiet

The world's greatest snorer
Was Barrington Brown.
His snores shook the windows
And rattled the town.

The people grew frantic
And fearful with fright,
And cried to each other,
"What happens tonight?"

They lullabyed softly
But who could ignore
The deafening noise
Of that terrible snore?

They tied up their heads
And their eardrums they bound,
But nothing could soften
That thundering sound.

They made a giant clothes-peg
And placed on his nose.
With one mighty snore
Like a rocket it rose.

So they all left town
In their cars and carts,
"We must be away
Before Barrington starts."

Then Barrington woke,
"Where's everyone gone?"
And then he turned over
And went snoring on.

Max Fatchen - from Songs for my dog and other people

1 What was the first thing the people did to deaden the noise of Barrington Brown's snoring?

_____

2 As the townspeople became more desperate which other two ways did they use to deaden the
   noise? _____

3 They made one more effort to deaden the snoring. What was it? Was it a success?

_____

4 Finally they couldn't stand it any more. What did they do? _____

5 Find synonyms in the poem for these words:

   desperate _____   powerful   _____   sang _____

   ear-splitting _____   turn a deaf ear to _____

6 Is there a snorer in your house? _____ Who is it? _____

   Describe the noises made by the snorer. _____

Science 2

Feel Your Heartbeat

Did you know that each time your heart pumps blood through your arteries and veins you can feel your **pulse**? Gently press two fingers on to the inside of your wrist on the thumb side. Use a timer or the second hand on a watch to count your **pulse rate** in beats per minutes **after** you complete each of these six activities. Don't forget to rest between each activity. Ask a grown-up to help you count the number of beats per minute.

A

Activity	Pulse Rate	Grown-up Pulse Rate
Sit still	_____	_____
Walk around room or garden for 2 minutes	_____	_____
Rest for 2 minutes	_____	_____
25 jumps on the spot	_____	_____
Rest for 2 minutes	_____	_____
Running on the spot for 2 minutes	_____	_____
Rest for 2 minutes	_____	_____
6 press-ups	_____	_____
Rest for 2 minutes	_____	_____
Clap hands	_____	_____

B 1 Which activity had the slowest pulse rate? _____

Why? _____

2 Which had the fastest pulse rate? _____

Why? _____

C Ask a grown-up to do the same activities as you did and take their pulse rate for each activity.

Are there differences? _____

Which are they? _____

_____

_____

_____

_____

Maths 9

Percentages %

A Complete this table. The first example is done for you.

$\frac{1}{2}$	50 out of 100	$\frac{50}{100}$	0.50	50%
$\frac{1}{4}$	out of 100			
$\frac{1}{5}$	out of 100			
$\frac{1}{10}$	out of 100			
$\frac{1}{20}$	out of 100			
$\frac{1}{25}$	out of 100			
$\frac{1}{50}$	out of 100			

B Find the **mean** for each of these five sets of data.

1   6, 2, 8, 6, 3 = ☐   2   14, 11, 15, 8 = ☐   3   8, 7, 9, 5, 6 = ☐

4   6, 9, 8, 7, 7, 5 = ☐   5   1.3, 2.4, 1.8, 5.8, 4.2 = ☐

C This square stands for 100.

What percentages do the following shaded parts stand for?

1   ☐ %

2   ☐ %

3   ☐ %

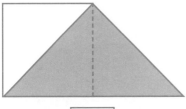

4   ☐ %

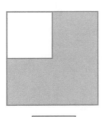

5   ☐ %

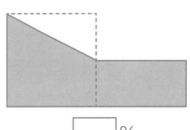

6   ☐ %

Language 10

Nouns to Adjectives

A Change these **nouns** into **adjectives** by choosing the correct suffixes from the list. Use your dictionary to check your spellings!

y	en	al	ular	ful	ish	ous	ly	able	ic

1 gold _____ music _____ poison _____ shower _____

2 skill _____ friend _____ accident _____ sun _____

3 nature _____ circle _____ wool _____ metal _____

4 fool _____ beauty _____ value _____ water _____

Analogies

B Complete these ten analogies.

1 man is to men as mouse it to _____

2 foot is to shoe as hand is to _____

3 happy is to sad as win is to _____

4 whisper is to shout as walk is to _____

5 here is to there as _____ is to that

6 food is to hungry as drink is to _____

7 uncle is to _____ as aunt is to niece

8 early is to _____ as near is to far

9 _____ is to wrist as foot is to ankle

10 descend is to depth as _____ is to height

Adverbs

C Complete each of the six sentences with an **adverb** which has the same meaning as the words in the brackets.

1 The plane landed at Manchester Airport [exactly on time] _____.

2 We are lucky because buses pass our house [at regular times] _____.

3 Our teacher speaks [in a soft voice] _____ but we can hear her very well.

4 The man on the market stall talked [all the time] _____.

5 The boys crept [without making a sound] _____ from the bedroom.

6 The survivors of the ship wreck were [in the end] _____ rescued by the lifeboat.

More Indirect to Direct Speech

D Change these five sentences from **indirect to direct speech**. Here is an example.

The girls said they were late because they missed the bus. [indirect speech]

"We are late because we missed the bus," said the girls. [direct speech]

1 The gardener explained that he was going to plant some shrubs. _____

_____

2 Gary's teacher asked him if he had read any of the Harry Potter books. _____

_____

3 Judy asked if I was going to the cinema on Tuesday. _____

_____

4 Grandpa complained that the cushion was much too hard for him. _____

_____

6 Dad explained that the laptop I liked was too expensive and I must wait to see how I progressed with our desktop. _____

_____

_____

Maths 10

A Find the **mean** for each of these five sets of data.

1 100g, 75g, 150g, 75g   = [ ]

2 27, 31, 46, 68, 38   = [ ]

3 60, 40, 55, 65, 45   = [ ]

4 £2.50, £3.25, £5.90, £4.35 = [ ]

5 1.25, 3.62, 1.94, 2.87, 1.82 = [ ]

Graph

B Answer these questions by reading the car ferry graph.

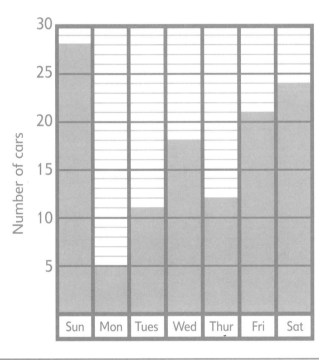

1 _____ cars used the ferry in the week.

2 The busiest three days were: _____, _____, and _____. Why do you think this was so? _____

_____

3 What is the average number of cars using the ferry each day? _____

4 _____ cars used the ferry on Monday. Give a reason for this. _____

_____

_____

5 Which three days had a combined total of cars equal to that on Sunday? _____, _____, and _____.

6 On Saturday the price per car is £12.50. How much is taken by the ferry in total on Saturday?

_____

Problems

C 1 One litre of ice cream fills nine tubs. How many litres would be needed to fill 135 tubs of ice cream? [ ]

2 $\frac{1}{2}$ litre of paint costs £2.85. What is the cost of $5\frac{1}{2}$ litres? [ ]

3 A boy's step is 45cm. How many metres will he walk in 360 steps? [ ]

4 How many pieces of card each measuring 10cm by 9cm can be cut from a sheet measuring 135cm x 70cm? [ ]

5 Sara has £10.80. If she spends £1.35 each day for one week how much will she have left? [ ]

The Old Man of the Sea

After a time I saw a little old man making signs to me to carry him on my back over the brook. Having pity on his age I did so, but when I would have put him down on the other side he twisted his legs so tightly round my neck that I fell to the ground half choked.

Though he saw how faint I was, he made no sign of getting off, but opening his legs a little to let me breathe better, he dug his feet into my stomach to make me rise and carry him further. Day after day, and night after night he clung to me, until by good luck I got rid of him in the following way.

Coming to a spot where, a few days before, I had left the juice of some grapes in a calabash, I drank the juice which, in the meantime, had become a very good wine. This gave me fresh strength, and instead of dragging myself wearily along, I danced and sang with right goodwill. The old man, seeing how lighthearted the wine had made me, signed to me to give him some. He took a deep drink and soon became so merry that he loosened his hold on my shoulders, when I tossed him off and killed him with a big stone, lest he should make me his victim once more.

Some sailors whom I met shortly afterwards said I was the first person they had known to escape from the man of the sea, who for years had been a terror to those obliged to visit the island.

From 'Sinbad the Sailor' in The Arabian Nights

1 What did the old man want Sinbad to do? _____

_____

2 Why do you think Sinbad decided to help the old man? _____

_____

3 What happened to Sinbad when he wanted to put the old man down? _____

_____

4 What did the old man do to make Sinbad carry him further? _____

_____

5 What effect did the wine have on Sinbad? _____

_____

6 Sinbad was helped by the old man drinking the wine. How? _____

_____

7 Find synonyms in the story for these words: for fear that _____

   weak _____   tiredly _____   friendliness _____

8 What happened to the old man after Sinbad tossed him off his back?_____

_____

9 Calabash means _____

Maths 11

Percentages %

A **per cent** means out of a hundred.
What per cent of each square is:
a) shaded? b) unshaded?

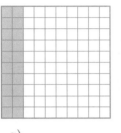 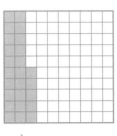 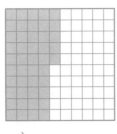 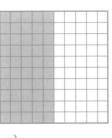 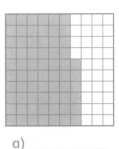

a) _____   a) _____   a) _____   a) _____   a) _____

b) _____   b) _____   b) _____   b) _____   b) _____

Mirror Letters

B Which of these eight words will look exactly the same when viewed in a mirror? List them below.

HANNAH   ABBA   TOT   DAD   TROT   MUM   BOB   TOUT

_____

C Find the **mode** for each of these five sets of data.

1 4, 7, 5, 4, 8, 4   = ☐   2 2, 9, 3, 9, 7, 7, 9   = ☐

3 6, 10, 14, 6, 11, 15   = ☐   4 21, 8, 11, 15, 11, 20   = ☐

5 63, 27, 15, 27, 63, 18, 26, 27   = ☐

Measuring Angles

D Use a protractor to measure these **angles**.

1

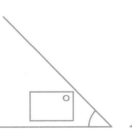 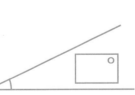 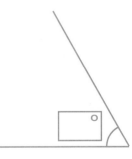

2

 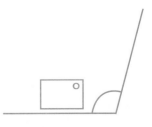

Language 12

About You

A Who is the oldest person you know _____
Describe him or her. _____

_____

What are your favourite sports? _____

_____

What do you enjoy at school? _____

_____

Do you have any pets? _____
If yes, write about them. _____

_____

How many people are in your family? _____
Who are they? _____

_____

When you are older what kind of work would you like to do? _____

_____

Do you enjoy reading? _____
If you do, which are your favourite kinds of books? _____

_____

Which is your favourite TV programme? _____
What is it you like about it? _____

_____

Describe yourself. Write a clear description so that you could be recognised easily by anyone who doesn't yet know you. Think about your height, the colour of your skin, hair and eyes.

_____

_____

_____

_____

Prefixes

B Think of a word that begins with the **prefix** in the first column. In the second column write your complete word. In the third column write its meaning. The first one has been done for you.

Prefix	Word	Meaning
cent-	century	a period of one hundred years
trans-	_____	_____
tele-	_____	_____
auto-	_____	_____
sub-	_____	_____
tri-	_____	_____
anti-	_____	_____

Maths 12

Area and Perimeter

A Measure the sides of these shapes in cm.

Find a) the **perimeter** b) the **area** of each shape.

Perimeter ☐ cm   Perimeter ☐ cm   Perimeter ☐ cm

Area ☐ cm²   Area ☐ cm²   Area ☐ cm²

Percentages %

B Find the value of:

1   10% of 70p   ☐ p   2   20% of 90p   ☐ p   3   5% of 50m   ☐ m

4   12½% of 72g   ☐ g   5   40% of 200m   ☐ m   6   20% of 250kg   ☐ kg

7   75% of 200m   ☐ m   8   25% of 320l   ☐ l

C

EVERMORE THEME PARK
Admission Charges

Family (2 adults + 2 children)	£14.50
Adult	£ 5.55
Baby (under 5)	Free
Child (under 11)	£ 2.50
Child (11–16)	£ 3.15
Pensioner	£ 3.50

How much will it cost to go into Evermore?

2 adults   _____   1 adult   _____

1 child (under 11)   _____   1 baby   _____

1 child (11–16)   _____   2 children (11–16)   _____

Total   ☐   Total   ☐

Change from £20 = _____   Change from £20 = _____

2 pensioners   _____   3 adults   _____

2 children (under 11)   _____   1 child (under 11)   _____

Total   ☐   Total   ☐

Change from £20 = _____   Change from £20 = _____

Schofield & Sims
HELPING CHILDREN TO LEARN

Schofield & Sims was established in 1901 by two headmasters and since then our name has been synonymous with educationally sound texts and teaching materials. Our mission is to publish products which are:

- Good value • Written by experienced teachers
- Extensively used in schools, nurseries and play groups
- Used by parents to support their children's learning • Educationally sound

MORE HOMEWORK BOOK 4

A brand new four book series designed to give children structured practice in: English - comprehension, spelling, grammar and usage; Maths - tables, the four rules of number, fractions, money, measurement and graphs; Science - living things, materials and their properties and physical processes. Answers are included in each book.

More Homework Book 1 - 0 7217 0879 X

More Homework Book 2 - 0 7217 0880 3

More Homework Book 3 - 0 7217 0881 1

More Homework Book 4 - 0 7217 0882 X

Schofield & Sims Key Stage 2 products for 7-11 year olds

Language and literacy workbooks

Key Spellings
Books 1-4
Pattern and sound based spelling activities and exercises to establish basic spelling skills.

New Spellaway
Books 1-4
A progressive series complementing the formal teaching of spelling. New patterns are consolidated through the 'look, say, cover, write, check' approach.

Springboard
Books 1-8 plus Introductory Book
English workbooks covering word construction, spelling, vocabulary, grammar, comprehension exercises and creative work. Age range 6-11.

Key stage 2 homework

Homework
Books 1-4
Workbooks that provide an excellent resource for work at home, with or without parental guidance. Each book includes a four page insert of answers for self or parental marking.

Maths and numeracy workbooks

Mental Arithmetic
Books 1-6 plus Introductory Book
Covers essential mental maths skills through 36 carefully graded tests in each book along with progress tests and diagnostic tests. Supported by corresponding series of Teachers' Books.

Times Tables
Books 1 and 2
Straightforward tables practice.
Book 2 covers x6, x7, x8, x9, x11 and x12 tables.
(Book 1 is for Key Stage 1.)

Posters

Sturdy, laminated posters, full colour, write-on/wipe-off, suitable for wall mounting or desk top use. Over 70 titles including the alphabet, numbers, colours, days, shapes, nursery rhymes, opposites, seasons, time, weather and our bodies.

Information

For further information about products for pre-school, Key Stage 1 and 2, please request our catalogue or visit our website at
www.schofieldandsims.co.uk

Authors   Andrew Parker
Cover Design   Curve Creative - Bradford
©2001 Schofield & Sims Ltd.

First printed 2001. Reprinted 2002, 2003
Printed by Hawthornes Printers, Nottingham

Schofield & Sims

Dogley Mill, Fenay Bridge, Huddersfield, HD8 0NQ
Phone 01484 607080   Fax 01484 606815

e-mail sales@schofieldandsims.co.uk

ISBN 0-7217-0882-X

9 780721 708829

Price £1.95
Key Stage 2
Age Range 7-11 years